THE FARM

to the lost farms of
Central Somerset

Nell Leyshon

THE FARM

OBERON BOOKS
LONDON

First published in 2002 by Oberon Books Ltd.
(incorporating Absolute Classics)
521 Caledonian Road, London N7 9RH
Tel: 020 7607 3637 / Fax: 020 7607 3629

e-mail: oberon.books@btinternet.com

A catalogue record for this book is available from the British Library.

ISBN: 1 84002 329 5

Cover photograph: Robert Jones

Cover design: Oberon Books

Printed in Great Britain by IBT Global, London

Characters

EDMOND
seventies, Grandfather

VIC
forties, Edmond's son

ROSE
late thirties, Vic's wife

GAVIN
twenty, their son

SUE
thirty-four, Market Researcher

The Farm was first performed at the Southwark Playhouse on 14 May 2002 with the following cast:

ROSE, Maggie Tagney

EDMOND, Brian McDermott

VIC, John Peters

GAVIN, William Bateman

SUE, Julie Hobbs

Director, Sean Aita

Co-Producers, Liz Leyshon for Strode Theatre Company and Harry Bucknall Productions

Designer, Marsha Roddy

Lighting Designer, Ned Dahl

ACT ONE

Scene 1

The kitchen, the main room in the house. There is a table and chairs, a fridge, an armchair, a television, and a window which looks over the home field. There are two doors. One to outside, with a coat rack next to it and a pile of Wellingtons, the other to the rest of the house.

Late afternoon, a wet and cold February.

It is nearly dark. ROSE is standing at the table. She has a box in front of her full of files and papers. She starts taking out some of the documents and looking at them. She shakes her head at each of them. Puts them back. She walks over to the window and looks out, then goes back to the box. She puts the box on the floor, in sight, then walks over to the fridge and opens it. The light goes on. It is nearly empty. She takes a colander full of lettuce out and puts it in a bowl on the table. The door opens and ROSE goes to help in EDMOND, whose body is stiff from arthritis.

EDMOND: Near bloody dark in here.

ROSE: (*Looking round.*) I didn't even notice.

EDMOND: I hate these afternoons. They go on so.

ROSE helps him into a chair. She turns on the lights.

ROSE: I know. Doesn't seem right, having lights on in the day. You have a good lie down?

EDMOND: I didn't sleep. My mind's playing tricks. Turning things over.

ROSE: Yeh. Well.

ROSE continues to get supper ready.

EDMOND: Vic not in?

ROSE : Not yet.

EDMOND: He's always in by now. He's working too hard.
Hardest I ever worked was that summer just after the war.

ROSE: (*Heard it before.*) Yeh.

EDMOND: There was summat about that summer. Like we
was alive again, had another chance. We was all mad
with it. (*Pause. Laughs to self.*) Hay was late, I remember
that. There was a girl that summer. End of one long hot
day. We lay down together in the sweet hay. She drank
some milk and I remember it stayed white on her lips
and I licked it off.

ROSE: Yeh.

EDMOND: Don't get that no more.

ROSE: No.

EDMOND: All gone now. They all drink that skimped
milk. No wonder they got rickets.

ROSE: What are you talking about?

EDMOND: Kids. Now.

ROSE: There's no rickets.

EDMOND: That's what they want you to think.

ROSE shakes her head. She starts putting supper on the table.

EDMOND turns and looks at the television which is off.

EDMOND: You don't wanna believe everything you hear.

ROSE: I don't.

EDMOND: Terrible things they say to make you think stuff.

ROSE: Who?

EDMOND: They.

ROSE: (*Lost.*) You hungry?

EDMOND: Made it hard, the hay being late. Up to our armpits, it was. And the ache in our backs from the scythe. We lay together in that hay. She had these three moles, under her eye. In a row. There's some things you never forget.

ROSE: Yeh.

EDMOND: Only – only I can't get it.

ROSE: What?

EDMOND: Her name. (*Slow.*) I can't remember her name.

The door bursts open and VIC enters. He kicks his wellies off and takes his jacket off.

VIC: What you doing, Dad?

EDMOND: Looking at the telly.

VIC: It ain't on.

EDMOND: Saves me having to turn it off. I like this telly. Big enough for me to see.

VIC: I reckon your eyes are going as well as your mind. (*VIC looks over at ROSE, who has unthinkingly wandered over to the window and is looking out onto the home field.*) What you doing, Rose? Rose?

ROSE: (*Turns round.*) What?

VIC: I said what you doing there, love?

ROSE: You'll be getting hungry.

VIC: You'll be stuck there one day. Daydreaming. You weren't like that last night. (*Gestures upstairs.*)

ROSE: (*Laughing*) Vic. You'll start your dad off.

VIC: (*Laughs.*) He doesn't know what I'm saying. Where's Gavin?

ROSE: I'm getting through the pork. Freezer's nearly empty.

VIC: How much you got?

ROSE: Can't be more than a few joints.

VIC: Right. I'll put a pig in next week.

ROSE: That'd be good.

VIC: What we got to eat tonight, then?

ROSE: Cold pork, potatoes, salad.

ROSE pulls the drawer out from the table and takes out knives and forks, counting four of each.

VIC: Salad?

ROSE: Yeh. Just a bit.

VIC: Why'd we want salad? It's winter.

ROSE: I got this stuff. You pour it on and mix it up. Tossing the salad, they call it.

EDMOND: What'll they think of next, eh? Tossing bleeding salads.

VIC: (*Laughs.*) Maybe that's why your eyes is going, Dad, eh?

EDMOND: (*Dirty cackle.*) What, tossing my salad?

Pause.

VIC: What's wrong with salad cream, Rose?

ROSE: For God's sake, I didn't say anything was wrong with salad cream. I just wanted to try it out.

VIC: We've always had salad cream.

EDMOND: I ever tell you, Vic, about that night down the Rose and Crown?

VIC: Only a hundred bloody times. (*To ROSE.*) Where is that Gavin? You never said.

ROSE: (*Getting plates out.*) Don't think he said where he was going.

EDMOND: No-one bloody listens to me.

VIC: Christ. I'm listening, Dad.

EDMOND: Right. It was that summer, the one after the war and we was all mad with it. Alive again.

VIC: Yeh yeh.

EDMOND: We was down the Rose and Crown one night, right? Right?

VIC: (*Too loud.*) Right.

EDMOND: Steady now. No need to shout. Any road, we'd had a few and we was all a bit oiled. This girl, right, a real red-headed beauty, walked in the bar and spotted me. She watched me for a bit, then wiggled her finger. Took me a minute to realise she was beckoning me. She made me follow her out the pub, through the yard and into the lavatories.

VIC: *Made* you.

EDMOND: Well, I didn't wanna offend her.

VIC: (*Laughs.*) No, Dad.

EDMOND: We went in one of the stalls – had to chase the goose out first – and she went and stood up on the bog – lid was down. Her head was among the ivy up by the cistern. Chain dangled over her shoulder. She pulled her skirt right up, had no panties on, showed me the lot.

VIC laughs.

ROSE sorts the table and gets the sauce bottle out.

ROSE: You shouldn't laugh, Vic. You encourage him.

VIC: Oh, he's all right.

EDMOND: I could still see to her, you know, like I did that night, don't you worry. (*Laughs.*) I can still toss the old salad.

VIC laughs, then stands up and stretches.

VIC: I'll go and call Gavin. Must be somewhere.

ROSE: He'll come in when he's done.

VIC looks at ROSE.

VIC: (*Cold.*) What you saying? Where is he?

ROSE: Christ, you're jumpy. I didn't mean nothing.

VIC: (*Stares at ROSE.*) I'll see if he's in the yard.

VIC leaves.

EDMOND: We got mint sauce?

ROSE: It's pork. You got to eat a good meal, build your strength up. You gonna come to the table?

EDMOND tries to get out of his seat, but struggles. ROSE helps him and walks him over to the table.

EDMOND: You don't wanna be worrying about my strength. Strong as a bull, I am. I'll still help, come haymaking. (*Breaks into song.*)

Come haymaking, come haymaking,
Come roll in the hay with I.

Pause.

Where's the beef?

ROSE puts a plate of pork on the table.

ROSE: *Pork.* It's pork.

EDMOND picks up the bottle of dressing, looks at it.

Pass your plate.

EDMOND: That girl down the Rose and Crown, you put me in mind of her.

ROSE: That's enough.

EDMOND: You ain't got no sense of humour.

ROSE: Not right now, no. Now pass your plate or you'll be licking it empty.

EDMOND: I once saw a cow lick the pattern right off a plate. I was at the gate, holding this plate where I'd just eaten off it. The cow reached over, stuck out its tongue and bang, all the pattern was gone. All them flowers and leaves just licked up.

ROSE: (*Smiles in spite of self.*) Just be quiet, will you.

ROSE puts food out. EDMOND picks up the bottle of dressing again. Turns it in his hand and stares at it.

VIC comes back in.

VIC: No sign of him.

ROSE: I'll keep it back.

VIC: Dunno where he's to. What's in that bottle?

EDMOND: Mint sauce.

VIC: It ain't green. What is it, Rose?

ROSE: Christ.

ROSE snatches the bottle off the table and puts it in the cupboard, brings out the salad cream.

Nothing.

VIC: We ain't the fancy types, us. You know that.

EDMOND: We ain't the tossing types.

VIC laughs.

ROSE: This is the twenty-first century now. Did you know that?

EDMOND: Twenty-first? It can't be.

ROSE: It is.

EDMOND: Reckon you got it wrong.

VIC: (*Through mouthful of food.*) This salad's bloody awful. Ain't right, eating it in the winter.

EDMOND: I ain't been alive that bloody long.

VIC: All this stuff grows in summer. Isn't natural to eat it in winter.

EDMOND: Summat's wrong with your sums.

VIC: Ain't right, eating out of season.

ROSE: (*Shouts.*) Shut up. Just shut up.

There is silence.

VIC: What was that about, then? Come on, what's brought this on?

Pause.

Jesus Christ. What's the matter with everyone?

Pause.

And where is Gavin? He's always here for his dinner. Look at you, Rose. Shape up.

EDMOND: I had this bull once, right big bugger he were.

VIC: (*Cold.*) Shut up, Dad.

EDMOND: This beef tastes queer.

VIC: Maybe 'cos it ain't beef. (*Sweet snarl.*) Let's try and guess, shall we, what it is. Honk, honk. Curly tail. Got it yet? You'll be in a home if you carry on like this. Nice big black woman in a uniform to change your nappy.

ROSE: Vic.

VIC: Dad, I got news for you, we ain't had cows down here for years. (*Slams table with fist and says words right in EDMOND's face.*) THE COWS ARE ALL GONE. DEAD. Got it?

VIC pulls back. EDMOND is oblivious to the tension, sat shaking his head.

They built a bonfire and heaped the cows on it.

EDMOND: I loves a bit of roasted beef.

Pause.

VIC: Sometimes I reckon you do it on purpose.

ROSE: Vic. He can't help it.

VIC: We got pigs now. Pigs.

ROSE: He's an old man.

VIC: (*Turns on ROSE.*) And who was it shouted? Eh? You're the one started it all.

ROSE: Can we just eat?

They eat.

Sound of the door.

VIC: (*Cheerful.*) Ah, here he is.

GAVIN walks in. He has on clean and ironed trousers and a shirt and tie.

(*Slow and careful.*) What's this? Carnival night?

GAVIN sits down.

What's going on?

ROSE: (*Passes GAVIN his plate.*) Here you are.

VIC: Are you all deaf all of a sudden? I said what's going on? Where you been?

Pause.

GAVIN: I got a job.

EDMOND starts eating again.

VIC: You already got a job. With me. What's going on?

GAVIN: I went and got myself a job.

ROSE: Vic, he had to go and…

VIC: (*Hand out to ROSE. To GAVIN.*) What job?

ROSE: Leave him alone.

VIC: (*To GAVIN.*) Come on.

GAVIN: The supermarket.

VIC falls back in his chair.

VIC: Oh Christ.

ROSE: We can't carry on like this. Something has to happen.

VIC sits forward. Speaks directly to GAVIN.

VIC: This is a farm, right? Right?

GAVIN: Yeh.

VIC: And you are my son. Right?

ROSE: Look if we –

VIC: So that means you work here on the farm with me. Understand?

GAVIN: The job's nights so I can still do the pigs with you.

VIC: That's not what I'm talking about.

GAVIN: (*Tentative.*) There ain't been enough for me to do.

VIC: Course there is.

GAVIN: There ain't the work there used to be.

VIC: One thing about farming, you always got things to do.

GAVIN: (*Firmer.*) I been scraping around for jobs.

VIC: (*Fake laugh.*) There's loads. There's the pigs.

GAVIN: I can still do the pigs.

VIC: They take up hours, the pigs.

GAVIN: There's no more milking anymore. That's what took the time.

VIC: And then there's the potatoes.

GAVIN: It's all set-aside.

VIC: And the hay. Who'll help with that?

GAVIN: I can do some of it and we'll get in extra help. It'll be cheaper.

VIC: You ain't listening.

ROSE: (*To VIC.*) Something had to happen.

VIC: (*Turning on ROSE.*) I spose this was your stupid idea.

GAVIN: (*Gently.*) Dad, things are bad.

VIC: You knew where he was.

GAVIN: Oh, for Christ's sake. Mum ain't even had the money to do the shopping.

VIC: (*Pushes chair back and stands up.*) She's got enough to buy that fancy bottle of sauce.

ROSE: It's not the bloody sauce.

VIC: (*Points at* EDMOND, *who eats obliviously.*) That's my dad and I've stuck by him, worked with him all these years. It's what we do. What we are.

VIC pushes his chair back in, rocking the table. He goes to leave.

ROSE: Vic.

VIC: There's no more to say.

VIC leaves.

Long silence.

ROSE: (*To GAVIN.*) I'm sorry.

EDMOND laughs. He puts his knife and fork down.

GAVIN: (*To EDMOND.*) What is it?

ROSE: I knew. I knew this would happen.

GAVIN: It's all right, Mum. (*To EDMOND.*) What you laughing at, Grandad?

ROSE stands and walks over to the window. She watches the following.

EDMOND: (*To GAVIN, surprised.*) You done the milking already, Vic?

GAVIN: Gavin, I'm Gavin. Vic's gone out.

EDMOND: Gavin, are you? How do you do? (*Puts hand out. GAVIN shakes it.*)

GAVIN: And your name? What's your name?

Long pause.

EDMOND: (*Puzzled. Slow.*) I just got this one picture in my head, Vic. It comes and goes. Moves like water. The scythe cuts the grass and the grass falls down and lays there, still. And there's one poppy red as blood. (*Looks over at ROSE, pleading.*) Who am I? I don't know who I am anymore.

Lights down.

Scene 2

The box is back on the table. EDMOND is dozing in his armchair.

ROSE sits at the table. SUE is unpacking her briefcase: she places some cans of soup and a clipboard on the table.

ROSE: You had a busy week?

SUE: Quite.

> *SUE sits down.*

How is he? (*Gesturing at EDMOND.*)

ROSE: He's with us some days.

SUE: Can't be easy for you.

ROSE: Well, no.

SUE: Shame. (*Picking up clipboard.*) Right. Who do you want to be today?

ROSE: Who was I last week?

SUE: Mrs Greenwood.

ROSE: Right. How about Mrs Palmer.

SUE: That'll do. (*Writes.*) Right, we're on chicken products this week. Cook-in sauces. Italians first: Tuscan sauce, Milanese sauce, Venetian Tomato Feast. None of those?

ROSE: No.

SUE: How about Indian? Chicken Tikka, Creamy Curry, Thai Chicken curry.

ROSE: That's not Indian. Not if it's Thai.

SUE: Must be from over there somewhere. So? Any of those?

ROSE: No.

SUE: Traditional sauces, then: Norfolk Casserole.

ROSE: No.

SUE: Mushroom and red wine.

ROSE: No.

SUE: Honey and lemon?

ROSE: No.

SUE: Mrs Palmer's on the fussy side. How about chicken pies? There's individual chicken and mushroom pies, chicken and vegetable pies, spicy chicken slice…

ROSE: I make my own pies.

SUE: So no pies. Right. (*Changes sheet.*) Now, these are the products that are really selling, you know since the beef thing.

ROSE: Is that what you call it? The beef thing.

SUE: Frozen breasts, legs and thighs. Chicken sausages, chicken burgers, chicken dippers, chicken nuggets, chicken fingers, chicken kievs, mini kievs, and there's these new ones, chicken lickens. Very popular with the younger age groups.

EDMOND: Chicken licken was gonna tell the king summat.

SUE: That's right. It's the story of the sky falling in, isn't it?

EDMOND: That's what's happening on this farm.

SUE: What's that?

EDMOND: The sky's falling in.

ROSE: Edmond, please. Sue doesn't want to hear this.

ROSE gets up and takes a drink with a straw in from the fridge, and passes it to EDMOND.

Here.

EDMOND: (*Raises carton.*) To Foxy Loxy who ate the lot.

SUE: You didn't say. Does Mrs Palmer buy any of those chicken products?

ROSE: What d'you do with all this stuff?

SUE: Send it off weekly to head office. I put it all together into one report first.

ROSE: A lot of work.

SUE: It's all right. I do it in the evenings. He finishes clearing up and I go in the study. Put some music on, you know. He helps me sometimes. He's good like that.

ROSE: What's he like, your husband?

EDMOND: I bet he's like a bloody bull.

SUE laughs.

ROSE: Edmond! (*To SUE.*) I'm sorry. He still gets so confused.

SUE: It's all right. He's harmless. I said you're harmless, aren't you?

ROSE rushes to fridge and gets out a cold sausage and gives it to EDMOND.

ROSE: There now, shush.

EDMOND: Sausage.

ROSE sits back down.

SUE: It isn't easy for you.

ROSE: No. No, sometimes it isn't.

SUE: My father-in-law died last summer.

ROSE: (*Reaches out and touches SUE's arm.*) I'm sorry.

SUE: He was such a sweet man. Used to squeeze my arm and say, 'My boy's a lucky man to have you.' My husband cried. I'd never seen him cry before. He said he hadn't given his dad any grand children.

ROSE: Did you want children?

SUE: We're still trying. Poor bugger's getting worn out. Yeh. He really cried.

ROSE: I've never seen Vic cry. Don't imagine I ever will.

ROSE looks down at the table. Upset. SUE notices.

SUE: Are you all right?

ROSE: I'm fine. I just.

SUE: I'm sorry. Have I said something?

ROSE: No. It's all right.

SUE: What is it, Rose?

ROSE: No. Nothing, Sue. It's all got on top of me. That's all.

SUE: You can tell me.

ROSE: No. Let's get on with it. Please.

SUE picks up the clipboard.

SUE: If you're sure. So is it no to the frozen chicken products?

ROSE: Better say yes to the breasts and thighs.

EDMOND: I'll drink to that.

The door opens and VIC walks in and looks at SUE.

VIC: (*To ROSE.*) What's she doing here again?

ROSE: *Vic.*

SUE: Hello.

VIC: Don't mind me. You carry on.

> *VIC sits down by EDMOND.*

ROSE: (*To SUE.*) I think we're nearly done, aren't we?

SUE: There's just the soups.

> *Points to cans.*

> *ROSE is reluctant in front of VIC.*

So if you had a choice of these, which would it be?

> *ROSE points to one of them. SUE writes it down.*

Can you say why?

ROSE: I like the colour. Nice and bright.

SUE: Lovely. (*Writes down.*) Now I'm going to say some words. See which ones you think apply to that tin of soup. Colourful. Well, you've already answered that. Fresh.

ROSE: Yes.

SUE: Appetising.

ROSE: Yes.

SUE: Delicious.

ROSE: I don't know. I haven't tasted it.

SUE: But from the look of it.

ROSE: Yes, then.

SUE: Home-cooked appearance.

ROSE: I can't tell that from the look of a can.

SUE: I see what you mean, Rose, but could something that came from that tin have a home-cooked appearance?

ROSE: I'm sorry. I don't know.

SUE: We'll skip that one, then. How about tasty?

ROSE: Is tasty different from delicious?

SUE: You're not supposed to *think*, Rose.

EDMOND: Tell us about your husband. What's his sperm count?

VIC laughs.

ROSE: God's sake, that's enough.

SUE: Don't worry for my sake. (*To EDMOND.*) Do you know, he puts me in mind of you. Nice strong man. Spec you were a goer, eh?

VIC: Don't you tease my bloody dad.

SUE: (*To VIC.*) He loves it. Bit of attention.

EDMOND: I ain't finished with women yet. I could tell you some stories…

ROSE picks one of the cans up quickly.

ROSE: I like this packet.

SUE: I like to see a bit of silver packaging on my cleaning fluids. (*Looks over at sink.*) You can get all that limescale off, you know. Special gel, squirt it on, then wipe it off. That's what I like, a product that does the work for you.

VIC: What a load of old bollocks.

ROSE: Vic, please.

SUE: Oh, he's all right. I've met worse than him. Right, we're done. I'll be back next week, then. (*Looks at VIC.*) That all right with you?

ROSE: (*To VIC.*) You're so rude.

SUE starts to pack up.

VIC: She don't care.

SUE: I don't think I do.

EDMOND: What you all on about?

ROSE: I'll have a cake and tea for you next week.

SUE stops still.

SUE: You're gonna *make* me a cake, aren't you?

ROSE: Of course.

VIC: Like we ain't got nothing else to think about.

SUE: I love coming here, you know. Shop ones just don't taste the same, do they? But then, who has time anymore, eh?

ROSE: Only me and my old-fashioned ways.

VIC: There ain't nothing wrong with our ways.

SUE: Did anyone say there was? (*Picks up case and starts towards door.*) I'll see you next week, Rose. Lovely to see you, Vic.

ROSE: I'll see you out.

Both leave.

VIC stands looking after them.

EDMOND: What was all that about?

VIC: Nothing.

EDMOND laughs to himself and shakes his head.

What? What is it?

EDMOND: Nothing.

Pause.

That summer after the war…

VIC: Oh Christ.

EDMOND: Hay tickled our armpits.

VIC: Shut up, you stupid old man.

EDMOND looks shocked.

VIC walks over to the table. Then to the window and cranes to try to see ROSE. Turns back to EDMOND.

On and on you go.

ROSE comes back in.

ROSE: Why do you have to chase everyone out?

VIC: Someone worth hanging onto, I might not.

ROSE: She's funny. She makes me laugh.

VIC: She's no business keep coming here.

ROSE: Just think of the money.

VIC: Doesn't exactly pay a lot.

EDMOND: That woman said summat. She said the sky was falling in. And I thought it was just an acorn. What's happening, son?

VIC: (*Short.*) Nothing, Dad.

EDMOND looks at ROSE.

EDMOND: Are you all right, Rose?

ROSE sits.

Don't you get upset again.

VIC: What are you on about?

EDMOND: She was upset, your Rose.

ROSE: He's confused.

VIC: I'm bloody confused. Maybe it's catching what he's got.

EDMOND: She was upset.

ROSE: He doesn't know what he's talking about.

EDMOND: All got on top of her. I don't know what's wrong with you lot. Her too. (*Towards door.*) That woman. You're all rushing around in a hurry. Ask yourselves why when you're only off to the grave anyway. Bloody slow down all of you and enjoy the view.

Silence for a moment.

ROSE goes over to the fridge and gets a plate out.

VIC: What's that?

ROSE: Gavin's.

ROSE goes to inner door and calls.

Gav! (*To VIC.*) He's got to eat. He's off, isn't he?

VIC: Off where?

ROSE: Work.

VIC: What work?

ROSE: Oh, Vic. Don't make him tell you again.

GAVIN enters in his uniform.

VIC watches GAVIN walk to the table and sit and pick up his knife and fork. ROSE fetches him a glass of water and sits at the table with GAVIN.

Long pause.

VIC: Someone better tell me I ain't seeing this.

GAVIN: Thanks, Mum.

ROSE: That's okay. How long will you be?

GAVIN: Not long today. It's just a couple of talks and that. Work out what I got to do.

VIC: So you're doing it then?

GAVIN: (*Not looking up.*) Yeh.

VIC: And the farm?

GAVIN: I'm doing it because of the farm.

VIC: If you cared about the farm you'd stay here and farm the fucking thing.

GAVIN: (*Calm still.*) Say what you like. I'm not changing my mind.

VIC: I might've known you'd come to summat like this. What with what you was like as a kid. Hanging on to your mother.

GAVIN: (*Loses it, half stands.*) You ain't gonna get away with –

ROSE: (*Stands. Shouts.*) Enough. Vic, don't start all that rubbish. And Gavin, you shut up.

VIC: I used to look at you and think Christ, here I am doing all this work just so –

ROSE: Shut up.

VIC: Just so that one day I can hand over the farm to that.

GAVIN: Well, did you never ask yourself if I wanted it?

ROSE drops her head.

VIC: Hand over the farm to that soft shit, who thinks he's too fucking clever for it.

GAVIN: I gave up school to farm it. I'm doing this stupid bloody job to help save it.

VIC: Too clever by half.

GAVIN: I'll do anything I can.

VIC: Oh yeah.

GAVIN: Just don't ask me to stand by and watch you lose it all.

VIC: You just want the easy money.

GAVIN: Listen. For once listen.

ROSE: Gavin. Eat and then go.

GAVIN stares at ROSE. Then nods.

Vic, you're making this really difficult.

VIC: Good.

ROSE: God, you can be a stupid man.

EDMOND: There ain't a moment's peace.

ROSE: It's all right, love.

EDMOND: Love, eh? You'll be wanting a legover, talking to me like that.

VIC laughs too loud.

I need to make a visit.

VIC: Jesus, Dad.

EDMOND: Now. Quick.

VIC looks at ROSE. ROSE shakes her head.

VIC: Oh bloody hell. Come on.

VIC helps EDMOND and they go through the inner door. ROSE sits back down with GAVIN.

GAVIN pushes his plate away.

GAVIN: I'm not hungry.

ROSE: You take too much notice.

GAVIN: I'll get something to eat later.

ROSE: I just wish things didn't get to you.

GAVIN: Look, I'd better go.

ROSE: Is it my fault? Are we too close?

GAVIN picks up his plate and puts it in the sink.

He doesn't mean half of it.

GAVIN: Sometimes I wonder if you can see him. You know, how he really is.

Pause.

ROSE: You're going to be late.

GAVIN: Yeh. I'll see you later.

ROSE: Okay. Just. Just try not to rise to it.

GAVIN: I'll try.

ROSE: (*Smiling.*) Good. Off you go then.

GAVIN: Right. (*Pause.*) Right.

GAVIN leaves. ROSE watches where he's gone, then turns and stares straight ahead of her, blankly. Lights down.

Scene 3

Later the same evening. EDMOND sits on his chair, wearing his coat. He has an old album on his lap and he turns over the pages. He turns one page and lifts it up to his face to read the words aloud.

EDMOND: (*Slow and careful.*) The Central Somerset Gazette. 1951. The crowds were lucky. The clouds broke and the sun shone on what they had been waiting for. The magnificent animals strode into the ring as if they owned it. (*Shakes head, lowers album to lap.*)

ROSE comes in. She walks over to the box on the table and stops. She looks at the box, walks back past EDMOND and closes the door.

ROSE: You cold? You got your coat on.

EDMOND: Bit nippy.

ROSE: (*Back to table.*) What's that you got? Oh, the old album.

ROSE looks through the letters in the box. Puts them down. EDMOND flicks through the pages, stops at one.

EDMOND: Old Billy won two years in a row.

ROSE looks up and smiles.

Beat the all-England champion one time.

ROSE: That's good. You're feeling well now, aren't you?

EDMOND: He was the strongest I had, Billy was.

ROSE: Didn't he ever scare you?

EDMOND: (*Laughs.*) They knew who was boss. Look at this one, Rose.

ROSE goes over, perches on the arm of the chair.

I remember that day. Clear as yesterday. Show people put us too close to the Jerseys and Old Billy got a bit frisky, tried it on.

They laugh.

ROSE: I know I'd have been scared.

EDMOND: Nothing to be scared of. Day before the show I'd wash Billy, scrub him all over, and he'd stand like a lamb. I used to go out and see him at night and he'd be pacing up and down, up and down, couldn't eat with his nerves. He was a good bull, Billy. I'd go out early the next morning, take the halter out, all clean and saddle soaped. The rope all white. Your Vic's mother'd scrub that rope till it glowed, that and the white coat.

ROSE: She was like that.

EDMOND: I'd rub his face as I put the halter on, smell him all fresh and sweet. His fur all curly. And then last thing, I'd Brasso the ring in his nose till it shone.

ROSE: Where's all those rosettes gone? You must've kept them.

EDMOND: Kept em all right. Out in the cattle sheds, all pinned up where Billy could see them. I went out one day and they was all ripped to buggery. We cleared out the sheds later, found the rats' nests, all lined in the coloured silk – red, blue and green.

ROSE: Looks like quite a crowd's there watching.

EDMOND: They always loved the bulls. Give em a thrill, I reckon.

ROSE turns one of the pages.

ROSE: Them necks. Massive.

EDMOND: Ain't nothing like it, great big thing at the end of the rope, you in charge. Best was, knowing you was the one what bred him. That if not for you, he wouldn't be there. (*Taps book.*) His mother Blacky, a good milker, she was. Lovely cow. I used to nestle in when I pulled her teats, she had a special smell about her. Christ, listen to me going on, soft bugger I am.

ROSE: They were your animals.

EDMOND: Used to like a tickle, Billy's mum. Just behind her ears, she liked it. Then she'd go and get that great big tongue out, lick my arm. Christ, felt like sandpaper taking the skin off. Mind, when you think on it, got to be strong enough to get the caul off a new-born calf.

ROSE: Could've licked the pattern off a plate.

EDMOND: Bugger, I saw a cow do that once.

ROSE: (*Laughs.*) I know. I'm teasing you.

EDMOND turns the page and sighs.

ROSE touches his shoulder.

Maybe you shouldn't keep looking at them, you know, if it makes you sad.

Pause.

EDMOND: People don't know what they're missing.

ROSE: It wasn't all easy.

EDMOND: Nothing's been the same since.

ROSE: Come on, maybe you should stop now.

EDMOND: It's all going.

Pause.

ROSE: I know.

EDMOND: Bulls, they don't even get the women anymore. The sperm man comes, draws the gloves on, shoves it in. My bulls, they had the pick of the women.

ROSE: (*Attempt at chirpy voice.*) I spec you did too. Now come on, you've warmed up a bit. Let's get your coat off.

ROSE helps him take his coat off. She drapes it over his knees.

That'll keep your bones warm. Come on, you have been feeling better tonight.

Pause. EDMOND closes the album and looks into distance.

EDMOND: I keep slipping, don't I?

ROSE: You're all right. There's nothing you should be worrying about.

EDMOND: I keep seeing it all open in front of me. These black patches. It's like it slips and I – I keep losing myself. What's happening, Rose?

ROSE: To you?

EDMOND: To all of us.

ROSE: I don't think you should… Look, it'll all be okay.

EDMOND: It's the whole thing that's going. You know that, don't you? The whole thing.

EDMOND looks down at the album.

Pause.

ROSE stands up and walks round the room. She goes to say something to EDMOND, but walks over to the box instead. She rifles through the letters again. EDMOND closes his eyes and looks as though he's about to drop off.

VIC enters and takes his boots off.

EDMOND: Bath and West Champion, I were.

VIC: Here we go.

ROSE: Vic. Leave him. He's having a good day.

VIC walks over to see what EDMOND is looking at.

VIC: You ain't got the message, have you? There ain't no more bulls.

EDMOND: (*Not looking up, loud.*) I know there's no more fucking bulls.

Silence.

VIC looks round the room. Sees the box on the table.

VIC: What's that doing on the table? Get rid of it.

ROSE: What are you saying?

EDMOND: Billy was a bloody fine bull.

VIC: Oh Christ.

ROSE walks towards the door.

And where are you going?

ROSE looks at him and leaves.

What's got to you, eh?

Long pause.

EDMOND starts looking through the album again. VIC walks over to the box and piles of envelopes. He flicks through them, shakes his head. Walks round the room. Looks out of the window. Then walks over to EDMOND and looks at the album, from a distance at first, then goes closer. EDMOND turns the page and VIC can't help being drawn in.

That is Blacky there, ain't it?

EDMOND: Yeh.

VIC sits on the next chair, they share the album.

You do remember her, don't you?

VIC: Course I bloody do, Dad.

EDMOND: Funny, your mother loved Blacky. Near as much as I did.

VIC: She loved all the animals.

EDMOND: Well, she were good with them.

VIC: Funny that.

EDMOND: All in her voice, some just have the way about them.

VIC: Yeh.

EDMOND: That's where you get it from.

VIC: Maybe.

EDMOND: Fact, I'm sure. I saw you once with, who was it? Big bugger. Wonky leg. Used to kick out in the parlour.

VIC: Jane.

EDMOND: That's the one. Jane. You told her, now, now, you said. That ain't what we do. And she bloody listened, like you'd given her six of the best.

VIC: Yeh. Well, I ought to get back out. Make a start on the pigs.

VIC stands up.

They'll be waiting for me.

EDMOND: Where did it go wrong? It was a fine farm then.

VIC: Look, I got to go.

EDMOND: A fine farm.

VIC: Yeh, well…

EDMOND: We never needed a lot. Just got on with what we was put here to do.

VIC: I can't stay here talking.

EDMOND: Sowed the seed. (*Turns page.*) Cut the grass, turned the hay. (*Turns page.*) Held buckets of milk for the calves, let them suck it off our fingers.

VIC: There's a lot to do.

EDMOND: And now it's going.

VIC: A lot to be done.

VIC walks away. He puts his boots on, but goes and stands by the window.

EDMOND: Will no-one listen to me?

EDMOND starts to turn over the pages of the album mechanically. Over and over. VIC walks over to the table.

Where's it gone, where's it gone, where's it gone…

VIC: Jesus, Dad.

VIC looks at the box and the pile of envelopes. He looks back at EDMOND.

EDMOND: Where's it gone, where's it gone, where's it gone…

VIC walks over to EDMOND and snatches the album off him. He throws it across the room.

VIC paces the room, then picks up the album and puts it on the table.

VIC: There it all is. There. (*Smacks hand down on album.*) All right?

VIC walks over and looks out of the window.

Silence.

ROSE comes back in.

ROSE sees VIC at the window, sees the album.

ROSE: What's going on?

No answer. ROSE takes the album and hands it back to EDMOND, who holds it but doesn't open it. She walks over to VIC and lays her hand on his shoulder, making him jump.

Vic. What's going on.

VIC brushes her off and walks over to the table. Sits on a chair. ROSE stands by the table. Puts her hands on the box. Long pause.

We've got to look at it.

VIC ignores her.

It's all in here.

VIC looks away.

Well, I'll make you bloody well look.

ROSE tips out box on table. The papers are held together with elastic bands.

(*Mechanical but forceful.*) This pile's the farm bills. Slaughterhouse, feed, garage for the gearbox. Timber yard. Wholesalers. This pile's the house things – water, sewage, council tax, electricity. (*Getting louder.*) Then there's the serious ones. VAT. Inland Revenue. Look.

VIC is still not looking. ROSE thrusts a pile in front of his nose.

Letters, registered bloody letters. Look at it, Vic. For God's sake. We can't pretend it's not happening.

VIC pushes her arm away and the pile falls to the floor.

VIC: Tell em. They have to wait.

ROSE: They have waited.

VIC: Just give them a tenner to shut them up.

ROSE: I don't even have a tenner to give them.

ROSE reaches in the box and takes out a ledger. She holds it to her chest.

VIC: What's the worst they can do? They just got to learn to wait.

ROSE: They can take the farm away.

VIC jumps up. Walks over to the window and back.

VIC: They can't do that. I'm only looking after it, keeping it for Gavin and then his boys.

ROSE: They can, Vic. It's the law.

VIC: Bollocks, that's what it is. Isn't it, Dad?

EDMOND continues to look at the closed album.

You ask him.

Pause.

Look, I'll tell you what I'll do, right. I'm gonna set the alarm earlier, Rose. Get an extra hour in in the mornings. Gavin'll do it with me too. The two of us. I'll get some more pigs. Fifty more pigs. A hundred more pigs.

ROSE: (*Not meeting his eyes.*) There's more in this pile.

VIC: Two hundred more if that's what's needed.

ROSE: (*Mechanical again.*) We haven't paid the PAYE for Gavin and now they say we should've been paying a different stamp for him. We owe them four years' worth of money for that.

VIC: Well you gotta tell em, Rose. He's my son and it's a private arrangement. Nothing to do with them. You understand. I wanna give my son work and give him a bit of money, I can bloody well do it.

ROSE: Vic.

VIC: Anyone'd think you was one of them, instead of my wife. *My wife.* You hear. (*Vulnerable.*) You got to tell em, Rose. They'll listen to you.

Pause.

ROSE: (*Calm.*) Vic, if we carry on doing nothing, we'll lose the farm.

VIC: And what ideas have you got, eh?

ROSE: There must be things we can do.

VIC walks round some more.

VIC: Like what? Go on.

ROSE: There's things other farmers are doing.

VIC: Bed and fucking breakfast. I'm not turning back sheets and frying bacon.

ROSE: What about the big outfits? We could sell to the suppliers.

VIC says nothing. He looks out of the window.

There must be things we could try. You can't do nothing, Vic.

VIC turns.

Come on, Vic. Look at all this. (*Gesturing at paperwork.*)

Long pause.

Say something.

Long pause.

VIC: (*Flat.*) People don't want what I can grow anymore.

ROSE: Course they do.

VIC: (*Flat and simple.*) They don't. I'll tell you what people want. They want their potatoes in boxes, all washed, all the same size. They don't care that they pay £1.99 for a box this big, that they could buy a whole sack off me for under three quid. They want their meat cheap, never mind how it's raised, how it's killed. They want to eat things their grandparents never knew existed, and they don't even want to wait till they're in season. They know nothing about food. (*Pause.*) Nothing I do has changed. I'm doing what's always been done on this piece of land. What he did, (*Pointing at EDMOND.*) what his dad did.

ROSE: I thought…

VIC: There's no use thinking. That's the way it is.

ROSE: But I could do something. Let me try.

VIC: I'll tell you what you can do. You can tell all these people I'm carrying on farming here like I always have. Like we always have. And if that's not good enough they'll have to come and get me. And I'll be in that window upstairs with the twelve bore aimed at them.

Pause.

ROSE: I know where it is.

VIC: You tell em, I'll be ready for them.

ROSE: I want you to move it.

VIC: No.

ROSE: I don't like it there.

VIC: It's my gun and I'll have it where I want.

ROSE: But not there. Not under our *bed*. (*Pause.*) Vic, with things as they are, we should have the gun locked up.

VIC: It's my gun. My bed.

ROSE: It's my bed too.

VIC: I was born in that bed.

ROSE: So was Gavin. He was born in it too. Vic, this isn't the time to have a gun hidden away.

VIC: I do what I want. I want my gun somewhere, I can have my gun somewhere.

ROSE: Vic –

VIC: So you tell them.

VIC pushes the paperwork off the table, scatters it all over the floor. Real sense of violence.

You tell them that's what I think of them.

ROSE: Don't do that.

ROSE grabs him and tries to stop him.

VIC: Get off me.

They struggle and VIC pushes ROSE to the ground.

Pause.

ROSE stays where she is.

ROSE: Do you know what you just did?

VIC: You shouldn't go on like that. It was you going on.

Pause.

I'm going out to work.

ROSE: But it's night-time, Vic.

VIC: I know.

He stares at EDMOND, who is watching, then puts his boots and coat on and walks out of the door.

ROSE touches her hair, looks at EDMOND, then stays on the floor and slowly and carefully gathers the paperwork up again. When she's bundled up what she can reach, she stands up and stuffs the rest of the papers in the box. She sits down and puts her head in her arms. Pause. Then ROSE lifts her head and looks at EDMOND, who looks at her.

ROSE: A pig costs sixty quid to raise and we get fifty-four quid for it. Vic's going to get more pigs.

ACT TWO

Scene 1

The room is dark. ROSE enters. She is humming. She goes to the box on the table and when her hands touch it she stops humming. Pause.

ROSE walks round the table and picks something up from the floor, puts it in the bin. She stands for a minute, then opens the fridge. The light goes on and shows it is still nearly empty. She walks up to the box again, touches it, walks to the window overlooking the home field. She stares out.

GAVIN comes into the room, still in his work clothes. He has some carrier bags.

GAVIN: You okay, Mum?

ROSE turns.

ROSE: Course. I'm fine.

GAVIN: Where's Dad?

ROSE: Out there somewhere. (*Pause.*) I know it's late. He's seeing to the pigs or something.

GAVIN: What you doing down here?

ROSE: Your Grandad was upset. I had to sit and talk to him a bit. He's not well.

GAVIN: No.

Pause.

Shall I put some lights on?

ROSE: If you like. (*GAVIN turns lights on.*) What's that you've got there?

GAVIN: Food. There's more in the car. I'll bring them in in the morning.

GAVIN opens the fridge and starts putting the food in it.

ROSE: There's a lot of stuff.

GAVIN: I know.

ROSE takes a tub of margarine and puts it on the table.

ROSE: I'll keep this out. I thought I'd make some cakes.

GAVIN: Now? (*Closes fridge.*)

ROSE goes to the cupboard and gets out flour and eggs.

ROSE: I been having trouble dropping off recently. I thought I'd stay up a bit later tonight. See if that helped. (*Starts organising and weighing ingredients.*) Mind, as soon as I do get to sleep, Grandad always seems to shout for me. Asks where he is, who he is. Poor old man. It's awful to see.

GAVIN: Can't we do anything for him?

ROSE: I don't see what we can do.

Pause.

GAVIN: You used to make those funny ones with wings.

ROSE: (*Smiles.*) Angel cakes. (*Remembers.*) You called them angle cakes for a bit. Couldn't get your mouth round the word.

GAVIN: I loved them.

ROSE: (*Laughs. Mixes margarine and sugar.*) You and your dad, you buggers used to try and eat them before I'd even filled them. I could have a go at some now if you like, they're only fairy cakes with the tops cut off. Angle cakes. Look at you, you great big thing. I can't believe you'll never be like that again, that it's all gone.

GAVIN: It's not gone. I'm here.

ROSE: You think when you're in the middle of it, it'll go on for ever.

GAVIN: Mum, should he be out there on his own?

Pause.

ROSE: (*Starts mixing.*) Crack those two eggs in the bowl for me.

GAVIN: Mum.

ROSE: I have to let him get on with it. I just – I don't know. (*Stops what she is doing, leaves hands still in bowl.*) I really don't know what to do. Sometimes I think I should do something, other times I think he's a grown man, it's his life and I can't watch him every minute. Can I?

GAVIN: No. Should I go and see him?

ROSE: It'd probably make it worse. (*Gets working on cake mixture again.*) Nice margarine this. Easy to work in. Pass the flour.

Pause while ROSE weighs flour and adds eggs to mixture.

GAVIN: One of the blokes at work.

ROSE: Yeh.

GAVIN: He's got a house. Rents out rooms.

ROSE stops. Waits.

He's looking for someone for one of the rooms. And I thought what with things being the way they are here. I'd still help out as much as I could.

ROSE: Is that what you want?

GAVIN: It's not to do with what I *want*. It's just – things are impossible here, aren't they, with Dad and that.

ROSE: And you said something to this friend?

GAVIN: I said I was interested.

Long pause. ROSE adds the flour.

ROSE: I've always told myself I'd let you go, Gavin. If you ever said you wanted to. But at the moment. Look, if you leave the farm now, you'll break his heart.

GAVIN: Oh come on, Mum. He can't stand me here. Can't look at me.

ROSE: It's only fear. He knows the mess the farm's in. He can't sleep. He's awake all night with it. Your father's not a bad man, Gavin.

GAVIN: You've spent half my life saying my father's not a bad man. So why can't he look at me? Why can't he stay in a room with me for more than a few seconds without starting up? I'm doing my best.

ROSE: It'll pass.

GAVIN: I can't live here with him. Can't even understand why you married him. You must've been desperate.

ROSE: That isn't fair.

GAVIN: I'm sorry. But you know what I mean.

Silence while ROSE finishes the mixing.

ROSE: I know why I married him. He was the only person I met who didn't bore me. I know he's not easy. Never was, he was terrible at school. (*Laughs.*) Famous for it. I was clever at school, like you, good at most things. I could have stayed on. The teachers wanted me to.

GAVIN: Why didn't you?

ROSE: (*Pause. Smile.*) Because I wanted to marry your dad. And no-one could believe it when I did. Not sure I believed it. But we rub along, most you can ask for. (*Pause.*) Look at this mess I've made here. The mixture's far too stiff. Maybe a drop more milk'd sort it. (*Puts milk in and mixes.*)

GAVIN: You've not got a lot in common.

ROSE: We have. We got you, the farm. He can be a good laugh.

GAVIN: On a good day.

ROSE: On a good day.

GAVIN: D'you never regret not finding out what you could've done?

ROSE: (*Looks at bowl.*) That's better.

GAVIN: You didn't answer.

ROSE: I know I didn't. Well, you were enough for me.

GAVIN: Me and *Dad.*

ROSE: I told you, he's not a bad man.

GAVIN turns away.

He just –

Pause.

He's his own worst enemy. Never says what he should. He'd never say how much he loves the farm. And how much he wants it to carry on. He and Grandad were so close when they worked together. He wanted that with you, to work with you like that. Always did from the day you were born. (*Tastes mixture.*) There. That's done. (*Pause.*) He has this thing, your dad. That he should die where he was born. On the farm, in his bed.

GAVIN walks over to the window and looks out.

He's just scared of losing it. He wants you to have it.

GAVIN turns round.

Pause.

GAVIN: But do I want the farm?

ROSE: (*Surprise.*) Don't you?

GAVIN: I don't know. I don't know if I could make it work. Not now, not a farm this size. (*Pause.*) I don't want to be stuck here, scratching at a living. But I can't bear the thought of losing it all either.

ROSE: No.

GAVIN: I never questioned it. Never thought there was a choice. I just followed him round, watching what he did. I used to come in and play with the farm set in here, setting up the milking parlour, driving the combiner. Stacking bales, rotavating. Just doing what he'd done that day. And now, oh I don't know. (*Pause.*) I don't want to regret anything. I don't want to look back and think what I could have done.

ROSE: Why don't you just wait till we see what happens? You may not have a decision to make.

GAVIN: How long?

ROSE: I can't see us lasting much more than a couple of weeks.

GAVIN: Weeks? Even with my money?

ROSE: That pays the interest. Nothing more.

GAVIN: How can you be so calm? Standing there making cakes.

Pause.

ROSE: I'm not calm, Gavin. I'm desperate.

Long pause.

What would you do. If the farm wasn't an option?

Pause.

GAVIN: I'd have to think about it.

ROSE: You'd go back to college, wouldn't you?

Pause.

GAVIN: Sometimes I think you know everything about me, everything I think.

ROSE: (*Smiling.*) You are my son, aren't you?

GAVIN: Course I am.

ROSE: No. I don't mean like that. I mean yes, I do know you. (*Pause.*) Well, this hasn't got the cakes baked, has it?

ROSE starts sorting some paper holders. GAVIN walks off and picks up the album. He sits on the floor out of sight of the door and looks through the pages.

VIC comes in. He doesn't see GAVIN.

(*Light voice.*) Pigs all right, love?

Pause.

VIC: I didn't mean to – do that.

ROSE: (*Trying to make him see GAVIN, but VIC is looking at the floor.*) It's late, getting on.

VIC: I didn't mean to do that. You know, for that to happen.

ROSE: Don't be silly, Vic.

VIC: It was just what you were saying. It was you going on.

ROSE: Sshhh, Vic.

VIC: A farmer needs a gun. I'm not moving it.

GAVIN stands up.

GAVIN: What are you talking about? What about the gun?

VIC: Oh Christ. Nothing.

GAVIN: What is it, Mum?

ROSE: Nothing. I don't know what he's talking about.

VIC: What you doing, hiding?

GAVIN: I wasn't hiding.

VIC: Trying to catch me out.

GAVIN: Why? What have you done?

VIC: Nothing. I've done nothing.

ROSE: Let's leave it. All of us. (*Hands up, pleading.*) Let's all stop and start again.

VIC: (*To ROSE.*) What are you doing down here at this bloody time anyway?

ROSE: Making cakes. They're nearly done.

VIC: You ain't gotta feed him. (*Pointing at GAVIN.*) He'll be eating at work now.

ROSE: Leave him alone. Stop it. Both of you. You have to stop this.

GAVIN: What you need to do Dad, is listen to yourself. For once in your life.

VIC: You speak to me like that and you can fuck off out of my house.

ROSE: He didn't mean it like that.

VIC: I decide how he means things.

GAVIN: Listen to what you're saying, Dad. Anyone'd think you hated us both.

VIC: And you're so perfect.

ROSE: Come on, Vic. You've got to get up early tomorrow. You need some sleep.

VIC: That's what you ought to do, get up early with me, do the real work.

GAVIN: I *am* getting up early. To help you with the pigs, then I'm going to work to earn some money. Real money. (*Stands up.*) I'm going to bed.

ROSE: But the cakes, Gav.

GAVIN: I'm sorry, Mum. You see now, don't you? How can I stay? (*Leaves.*)

Pause.

ROSE: Every time. (*Slow and careful.*) Every time I think I'm getting somewhere, I slip backwards. Well I'm not going to stand here and watch this anymore.

ROSE picks up the bowl of cake mixture. Starts tipping it in bin. Ends up tipping in the bowl as well.

VIC: Don't. (*Rushes forward and tries to grab it.*)

ROSE leaves the room.

VIC stands still. Silence.

VIC walks over and picks up EDMOND's album. He opens it, then closes it and places it on the table. He clears up the few things left on the table and leaves the room.

Scene 2

Late afternoon. There's the remains of tea on the table.

ROSE has a similar uniform to Gavin's on her lap and she strokes it. EDMOND is in his chair, a glass in his hand. SUE has a glass and a sherry bottle. Her packages and clipboards are out on the table.

SUE refills her glass. She walks over to ROSE.

SUE: Come on, Rose. You're getting left behind.

ROSE: You'll have me turn up drunk on my first evening.

SUE: Only a bit of fun. Nothing wrong with fun.

EDMOND: What about me? You wouldn't forget an old
　　man, would you?

SUE: (*Laughs and goes over to fill his glass.*) How could I
　　forget the bull man, eh?

EDMOND: That's the one. (*Pats knee.*) Here, come and sit
　　on here. I ain't felt a good bit of rump since the cows
　　went.

*SUE giggles and walks back over to the table. She picks up
the clipboard.*

SUE: We're not doing too well here, are we? I blame the
　　drink. Right. Let's get to it. We're on tomato products
　　today, Mrs Webber.

ROSE: (*Straightening up, paying attention.*) Right.

EDMOND: I grew my own tomatoes, never missed a year.

SUE: Tins first. Okay?

ROSE: Okay.

SUE: Whole?

ROSE: Yeh, I buy those sometimes, when we've eaten ours.

EDMOND: My Vic grows them in the greenhouse. Same as
　　I used to.

SUE: Lovely. What about chopped?

ROSE: They cost more.

SUE: Ah, but you don't have to chop them.

ROSE: No.

SUE: Chopped with garlic?

ROSE: No.

SUE: Chopped with basil?

ROSE: No.

SUE: Chopped with basil *and* garlic?

ROSE: No.

SUE: Organic?

EDMOND: What are you on about, Missus?

SUE: No to organic?

EDMOND: I used to put the dried-up tops in my mother's bed.

ROSE: No to organic.

EDMOND: Looked like spiders.

SUE: (*Marking on clipboard.*) Tomato puree?

EDMOND: She'd give me a clout.

ROSE: Yes.

SUE: What about sun-dried tomato puree?

ROSE: Never heard of it.

SUE: It's made from sun-dried tomatoes.

EDMOND: What's them?

SUE: Dried in the sun. That's why they cost more, someone's got to lay them all out, pick them all up.

EDMOND: You're making it up.

SUE: I'm not, honest. It's on this sheet.

EDMOND drains his drink and holds his glass out. SUE goes to stand up to fill it.

ROSE: He's had enough. And I've got to go out.

EDMOND: (*To SUE.*) Come on, Mrs Tomato Lady.

SUE: (*To ROSE.*) Come on, Rose, he's all right. Having a ball, aren't you, Champion shower? (*Fills his glass.*) D'you know, I done this so many times this week, reckon I got the rest of it in here. (*Taps head.*) You check me off on the sheet, Rose. (*ROSE picks up sheet.*) Sun-dried tomatoes in a bag.

ROSE: Yep.

SUE: Sun-dried tomatoes in oil.

ROSE: Yep.

SUE: Sun-dried tomato and herb marinade.

ROSE: Yep.

SUE: (*Speeding up as goes through list.*) Tomato ketchup, that's squeezy bottles or glass bottles, reduced calories, organic. Chutneys. Tangy tomato pickle, tomato chilli chutney, fresh tomato salsa. Then there's tomato ketchup crisps, ovencrisp sun-dried tomato and herb crisps. Tomato juice. Organic and cheap. Cajun chicken tomato sauce. Chunky spicy tomato and pepper sauce. Tomatoes stuffed with olives. No. Olives stuffed with tomatoes. Then at the bottom there's the fresh stuff. Ready washed tomato salad, slicing tomatoes, beefsteak tomatoes, plum, midi-plum, mini-plum, cherry tomatoes, family pack, vine tomatoes – five times the price, got to pay for the stalk. Well, did I miss any?

ROSE: Not bad. There's another sauce.

SUE: Tomato, tomato. (*Pause.*) Pilchards in tomato sauce? No, that's fish. That's next week.

ROSE: Chinese.

SUE: Don't tell me. (*Pause.*) Chinese tomato, ginger and garlic stir fry sauce.

ROSE: What about the new lines?

SUE: Easy. I have to ask would you buy any of the following tomatoes if you saw them. Yellow tomatoes, green tomatoes, striped tomatoes. And we've got a new line of tinned tomatoes: *Herbes de Provence.* 'The smell of freshly trodden on wild herbs.'

EDMOND: We just have them fresh from the greenhouse. The smell clings to your fingers.

SUE: That's what I love about it here. Everything's so simple.

ROSE: That's us. Just a bunch of simple people.

SUE: Home-made cakes. A hot dinner every night. Tomatoes that taste of something.

ROSE: You'd be bored soon enough. (*Holds up uniform.*)

SUE: No. I'd love it. Here, you should try that on.

ROSE: Now?

SUE: Why not? You'll be in it tonight. Come on. Let's see what you look like.

ROSE steps into her uniform, pulls it on top of her clothes while SUE pours more drinks.

If they could see me now, eh? Market researching.

ROSE: Would they sack you?

SUE: I don't reckon I'd care. (*To EDMOND.*) Having a ball, aren't we? (*To ROSE.*) You look lovely, Rose. Colour suits you.

SUE pulls a chair out and puts it by the table.

Right. We're gonna give it a go, give you some practice for tonight. You sit there. You're at the checkout. I'm coming through.

ROSE: I'm the express checkout. Ten items only.

SUE: The lonely person's checkout.

SUE passes ROSE the products and ROSE passes them in front of an invisible scanner. She beeps.

ROSE: Lovely weather we're having. Beep.

SUE: Christ, Rose, they don't talk to you. You got to have a face like this.

ROSE: Can I help you pack?

SUE: They don't do that either. You'll have the sack the first day, raising customers' expectations.

ROSE: That'll be two thousand three hundred pounds and forty-nine pence.

SUE: That all? I got a ten pence off voucher from the back of the bog roll packet.

ROSE: So handy, aren't they? (*Passes voucher in front of scanner.*) That'll be two thousand three hundred and thirty-nine pence in that case. Not bad for a day's shopping.

SUE: Keep me going till tomorrow at least.

ROSE: Would you like any cash back, Madam?

SUE: Why not? An extra five thousand. For the weekend.

EDMOND: You two are nutters.

SUE: We got mad cows' disease. (*Pause.*) We're mad cows.

Pause. ROSE stares at her.

ROSE: You can't say that. Not down here.

Pause.

You're terrible.

SUE: (*Laughing.*) I know.

ROSE: (*Laughing.*) Jesus, Sue.

GAVIN walks in from the yard. He has his boots and jacket on.

GAVIN: What's going on?

SUE: Ah, hello young Sir. (*Picks up clipboard.*) Now, I'm doing a bit of research, would you mind answering a few questions? I'm on tomatoes at the moment, and would appreciate it if you'd answer yes or no to the following. Would you buy tomatoes if they were shapes like arses, with ruddy great cracks down them?

GAVIN: Definitely.

SUE: How about our new hairy tomatoes? Each has a small wig which is detachable.

GAVIN: Don't they catch in the throat?

SUE: How about our pesticide range? Guaranteed one hundred percent flammable, can be used as fire lighters. Coated with five layers of chemicals. Guaranteed completely tasteless. Never go off. The busy housewife's favourite. No need to ever shop again.

ROSE: You are mad.

SUE: Mad, madam? Mod, modom, mid, midam.

VIC enters from yard.

Now let me see if you'd be interested in purchasing one of our special, top-secret giant tomatoes…

ROSE's hands fly to her uniform.

VIC: Well this is a fine fucking thing.

SUE: We were just messing about. Having a laugh.

VIC: No. No you don't have to say nothing. There ain't nothing to say is there? I'm out working my fucking bollocks off and you lot's in here drinking yourselves stupid.

SUE: It's all my fault.

VIC: Bringing your fancy ways down here. Rubbing my nose in the shit.

SUE: I wanted Rose to have a laugh. That's all it was.

VIC's sarcasm is to protect himself, but it breaks down through the following.

VIC: But look, I don't want you feeling bad. Don't want to spoil your fun.

GAVIN: Dad – no harm was meant.

VIC: No. I don't want any of you feeling bad. In fact, I've got a good idea. I'll give in. Sell the farm. No. Fuck it. I'll give it to them. They can pull down this old house, plough up the yard. Build a whole estate on the home field. Another in the five acre. Nice little houses with neat little gardens. And best of all they could have a nice big supermarket to feed them all. What d'you think?

ROSE: Vic, please. It was just a laugh.

VIC: You could all work in there in those lovely nylon uniforms. (*Looks at GAVIN.*) You too. No more helping me out there. You could all dress up and laugh away behind your stupid fucking tills.

ROSE: I needed a laugh.

VIC: And you can watch people buying all that stuff. Cheap meat from abroad. Half-grown vegetables.

GAVIN: Look, Dad.

VIC: And I'd have nothing to worry about. I could stop spending my nights walking the farm, worrying myself sick. See you can't all be here laughing when this is happening to me. It ain't a game. This is my land. My life.

ROSE walks towards him.

Don't you come near me.

GAVIN steps towards VIC.

None of you.

GAVIN: All right. You've said it now, Dad.

VIC: (*To ROSE.*) What's the idea – you going to work with Gavin? (*Calm, direct, as though talking only to ROSE.*) Me and this farm obviously ain't good enough for you.

ROSE: That's not fair, Vic.

VIC: I should let you go.

ROSE: No.

VIC: You and Gavin. You don't need all this, do you? You'd be better off without it.

ROSE: You don't know what you're saying.

VIC: I'm just this stupid bastard, aren't I? Getting up in the dark, putting the hours in, and all for nothing. No-one wants to know it any more.

ROSE: No. You're wrong.

VIC: See, Rose, I know. We're living in a dead world down here. A dead world. And there's nothing I can do.

Pause.

VIC turns to leave.

ROSE: Vic, wait. Don't go like that.

VIC leaves.

Silence.

ROSE: I have to go.

SUE: I'm so sorry. That was my fault.

ROSE: No. It's all right.

SUE: How bad is it?

ROSE: Weeks.

SUE: And you'll lose it all?

ROSE: Yeh.

SUE: I had no idea.

ROSE: Well that's just how it is.

SUE stands up and starts gathering her things together.

ROSE looks over at GAVIN. They talk to each other as though they are alone.

GAVIN: I'll stay, okay, till we know.

ROSE: That'd be good.

Pause.

GAVIN: Where's his gun?

ROSE: Under our bed.

Long pause.

GAVIN: I should move it, shouldn't I?

Pause.

ROSE: I don't know.

Pause.

No. I don't know.

GAVIN: I should go and see him.

ROSE: No. It has to be me. I'll go and see him. (*Looks down at uniform.*) Then I'll go to work. Try to earn some money.

GAVIN: I'll stay here and look after Grandad.

ROSE: Okay.

SUE: Can I stay and clear up for you?

GAVIN: No. I'll do that.

ROSE: Thanks, Gav.

Pause.

SUE: You see, I didn't know. I wouldn't have…

ROSE: No. I know.

SUE: I'm so sorry.

ROSE: It's okay. Look, I'd better go and find him.

SUE: Do you want me to come back next week?

ROSE: I don't know. I don't think I know anything anymore.

SUE: No.

ROSE: Right. I'll go and find him, then. I'll see you in the morning, Gavin.

SUE goes to say goodbye but ROSE leaves quickly.

Long pause.

SUE: I didn't know. I really didn't know.

SUE clears a plate and places it in the sink.

GAVIN: It's okay. It doesn't matter.

SUE: If I'd known.

GAVIN: I can do this, you know. There's no need.

SUE: No. I really want to.

GAVIN: Whatever.

SUE: Your dad, I thought he'd –

GAVIN: (*Sharp.*) Leave it.

> *Long pause.*

SUE: Right. Well maybe I'll just go.

GAVIN: Yeh.

> *SUE leaves.*

> *GAVIN covers EDMOND with a coat.*

> *GAVIN leaves the room. Lights down.*

Scene 3

Later. EDMOND is still in the chair, the coat over him. It is dark. He wakes up suddenly and starts shouting.

EDMOND: Help. Someone help me.

> *Pause.*

Where are you?

> *Pause.*

Where am I?

> *GAVIN enters, quickly. He turns the lights on and runs to EDMOND and crouches next to him.*

GAVIN: It's okay. I'm here.

EDMOND: Someone has to help me.

GAVIN: It's me, Gavin. Look at me.

> *EDMOND looks at him.*

EDMOND: Who?

> *GAVIN sits on the arm of the chair.*

GAVIN: You're all right. It's all all right.

EDMOND: All all right.

> *EDMOND looks up at him as though he has never seen him before.*

Who are you?

GAVIN: I'm Gavin, just Gavin.

EDMOND: Did you know, I was a Champion Shower.

GAVIN: Never. What did you show?

EDMOND: Bulls. Great big bulls on white ropes.

GAVIN: Go on.

EDMOND: No-one listens to me.

GAVIN: I'm listening.

EDMOND: I did love my bulls.

GAVIN: Course you did.

EDMOND: Those ropes, they were always white as white.

GAVIN: White as snow.

EDMOND: Whiter.

GAVIN: Whiter than snow.

EDMOND: Whiter than that.

GAVIN: Whiter than whiter than snow.

EDMOND closes his eyes and seems to be dropping off to sleep, but he opens them suddenly.

EDMOND: Oh, Vic.

GAVIN: Gavin, I'm Gavin.

EDMOND: I love this farm, Vic.

Pause. GAVIN looks round, tentative before answering.

GAVIN: I know you do.

EDMOND: I worked hard to keep it. Got up in the dark, got the cows in in the dark, milked in the dark. Up all night ploughing, cos it's the only time I had.

Pause.

I know you love this farm too, Vic. Same as I love it.

Pause.

Can we walk the farm?

GAVIN: It's night. Dark. We can't go out now.

EDMOND: I don't need to go out. (*Taps head.*) It's all in here, the whole lot of it. We'll start in the yard, go past the old roller, the red tractor. Smell the hay from the barn how it comes in on the wind. Go out the yard, down the home track and lean on the five bar, look at the home field. Can you see it?

GAVIN: (*Quietly.*) Yeh.

EDMOND: Can you see it, Vic?

GAVIN: I can see it.

EDMOND: Look at that clump of docks there, by the old tractor tyre, got to see to them before they seed. Hedges want laying, and time we cleared out the rhynes. Let's wander down to the ten acre, look – soil's freshly turned over, loose from the spuds. (*Laughs.*) I can still feel the old ache in the back from gleaning the last of them. (*Pause. Panicky tone.*) What's the next field, Vic? Vic, what's next?

GAVIN: The oak field.

EDMOND: Times I've ploughed round that tree.

> *As EDMOND speaks, VIC enters through the inner door. He stands quietly and listens.*

Round and round, year after year. The trunk thickening. Let's go on down onto the flat land, into the twenty acre. Here we are. The swallows are high up, black shapes moving against the blue. The air smells sweet. I can smell the pollen from the grasses. (*Pause.*) There's the parlour in the corner. (*Gentle laugh, delighted.*) I can hear them, hear their hooves, the sound of their breathing and snorting, the jostling to come in. To be the first. And who's this? Mary. Comes into the stall, stands with the off hind resting, gets her head in the trough, then she turns her head and looks at me. Always Mary first for me. Who is it for you, Vic? (*Looks at GAVIN, but VIC steps forward and answers.*)

VIC: Jane.

EDMOND: (*Laughs.*) Jane and that wonky leg. You watch out, Vic. (*Still talks to GAVIN.*) You watch out Vic she don't kick out and get you a cracker. (*Pause. VIC and GAVIN look at each other.*) Who's this now coming? Patch.

> *VIC comes closer. He taps GAVIN on the shoulder and GAVIN stands. They change places during the following.*

She's early today, look at that, bright red scratch on her nose. Nice black nose, Patch. Rubs it on me, spit hanging down. Moves her legs so I can get the cups on and lets down the milk and it streams out. Sound of her eating. Always been a noisy eater. Who you got now after Jane?

VIC: Bertha.

EDMOND: You got Bertha. Still the same is she, that tongue hanging out. That nick in her ear?

VIC: Yeh.

EDMOND: Ah, who's this coming in now for me? (*Pause.*) It's (*Long pause.*) – who is it, Vic?

VIC: What's her face like?

EDMOND: Looks like she's got a white blaze down her face. She's always in after Patch. Likes to grab my sleeve and give it a chew. Her name – I can't remember her name. I know all their names. All the names. All the cows I ever had. But I can't remember this one.

Long pause.

Vic.

VIC: I'm here.

EDMOND: I wish you'd lie me down, Vic, in the hay.

VIC looks at GAVIN. Pause.

VIC: I'll lie you down.

VIC takes EDMOND's arm.

Come on.

VIC takes EDMOND out of the room.

GAVIN straightens EDMOND's chair and the room. He stands and waits, nervous.

VIC returns. He goes to the sink and washes his hands, then splashes water on his face, dries himself.

Long pause.

GAVIN: I wanted to say sorry, Dad, about all that earlier.

VIC: Right.

GAVIN: It was just a laugh. No-one thought –

VIC: I said it's all right.

Pause.

GAVIN: So. The pigs all done?

VIC: Yeh. (*Pause.*) Your mother's gone to work.

GAVIN: She said.

VIC: Right. And you're going in tomorrow.

GAVIN: Yeh.

VIC: You'd better get some sleep then.

GAVIN: Yeh. You coming up too?

VIC: I'll wait up for your mum.

GAVIN: You'll be all right?

VIC: I wouldn't worry – I can't shoot myself tonight –
   Dad'll be calling out for me. (*Laughs.*)

GAVIN: (*Laughs nervously.*) Right.

VIC: So you'll go to work.

GAVIN: Yeh.

VIC: I'll see you before you go.

GAVIN: Yeh.

VIC: Right. (*Pause. GAVIN goes to leave.*) Maybe you can give
   me a hand. There's a few things.

GAVIN: Course I can. Anything.

VIC: Yeh. There's just a few things. An extra pair of hands'd be a help.

GAVIN: I'll get up early.

VIC: Don't want you going in smelling of pigs.

GAVIN: I'll have time for a wash. If they don't like it –

VIC: (*Gentle laugh.*) Yeh.

> *Pause.*

GAVIN: Right. I'll go on up then. I'll see you.

VIC: Yeh. See you.

> *Pause. GAVIN goes to leave again.*

I just.

> *GAVIN stops. Waits.*

I wanted you to have it. That's all.

> *Pause while the two men look at each other.*

GAVIN: I know, Dad. I know.

> *GAVIN leaves.*
>
> *VIC settles down in EDMOND's chair and waits.*
>
> *Lights down.*

Scene 4

Dawn. VIC is in the chair, sleeping. EDMOND's coat on him.

ROSE enters in her uniform. VIC slowly wakes up. Long pause. All the following is gentle and slow.

ROSE: You didn't have to wait up.

VIC: No.

ROSE: Grandad all right?

VIC: Sleeping.

ROSE: Right.

VIC: And Gavin's in bed.

ROSE: Yeh.

VIC: He's getting up early. Helping me in the morning.

ROSE: Oh. (*Pause.*) Good.

VIC: Yeh.

> *Pause.*

> So?

ROSE: So I sat in the car in the car park. Watched the clock on the dashboard.

VIC: You didn't go in?

ROSE: No. I don't know. I just couldn't. I sat there and waited and just thought. Then I went to see Sue.

VIC: Why?

ROSE: I knew she was upset. It wasn't really her fault, what happened. Oh I don't know. It just seemed the right thing to do.

VIC: Right.

ROSE: (*Flat delivery for following.*) It took me a while to find it. She looked surprised to see me, but she opened the door and I followed her up the stairs. There were four doors on the landing, all closed. She opened one of them and I followed her into the room. It was spotless. There was a gas fire on in the fireplace, ornaments on the mantelpiece, little china dolls.

There was a sofa in the corner of the room. It had one of those throws over it and some cushions, but I could tell it was a bed really.

She asked if I wanted tea, and I said I did and she walked to this big cupboard and opened it. There was a microwave in it, a tiny sink. A two-ring cooker with a camping gas cylinder underneath. She put a saucepan of water on to boil and took out the only two cups she had.

Pause.

There was a washing up rack and in it was one plate, one bowl, one knife, one fork, one spoon.

I waited till she made the tea, then we looked at each other. I know, she said. All that, I said. The husband, his father dying, trying for a baby, the house. (*Pause.*) Yes, she said. Everything.

ROSE shakes her head. Stands up.

ROSE takes her uniform off as she says the following. She is wearing a slip underneath.

I sat in the car just outside the village for hours. Then I went for a walk in the dark. Through the back lanes and up the hill. I sat on the wet grass and watched day break over the farm.

Pause.

There were no clouds. Just this big fat sun. And I thought of all those times I'd looked down on the farm from up on the hill. First time I could remember was before I started school. I went up there with Gran and picked cowslips. They were everywhere then and we gathered them in a big yellow ball and tied them with string.

I could remember another time on my own, when I was about ten. I could remember looking out over the land and seeing the farm and the shape of the fields and the rhynes. Like I was looking down on a map.

And then with you, that time we were up there and you had your gun.

Pause.

VIC: I got a few rabbits that day. (*Pause.*) It was a hot summer.

ROSE: The grass was all dry.

VIC: Yeh.

ROSE: The grass was all dry and we lay there.

VIC smiles as the memory returns.

VIC: That time.

ROSE: There was one other time. The day of our wedding. I got up early, before everyone else and went up there. Just to be on my own for a bit. I looked down on the farm and thought that'll be my home from now on.

Long pause.

ROSE holds the uniform out to VIC.

VIC takes the uniform.

I sat on the hill this morning, like all those times, and thought even if we lose the farm, we'll have been here. We'll have looked after it, you'll have done what you did. Made your mark. And I thought as I sat there that whatever happens, wherever we end up, I've never regretted any of this. That's all. That's all I wanted to say.

Lights down.